addic

New Understanding • Fresh Hope • Real Healing

$19.99
ISBN 978-1-60402-381-7

Published and distributed by
The Institute for Addiction Study
Salt Lake City, Utah

Copyright©2007 by The Institute for Addiction Study
All rights reserved. No part of this work may be
reproduced without written permission of the publisher.
Intellectual property of The Institute for Addiction Study

Appreciation and Acknowledgement

We give special thanks to Kevin and Sydney Knight who through their generous support and genuine compassion for those affected by addiction made this book possible.

We also give our thanks and appreciation to Cody Knight and Kim Griesemer for their support and help in bringing this book together.

Table of Contents

Introduction

Chapter One: 1
Addiction: Is it Really a "Disease?"

Chapter Two: 9
Addiction, Stress, and Dopamine

Chapter Three: 23
Helping the Addict Accept Treatment

Chapter Four: 31
The Problem with Punishment

Chapter Five: 37
A Group of Addicts We Don't Punish

Chapter Six: 41
People Get Sober All the Time

Introduction

This book and its companion audio CD explores the answers to a series of questions I asked Dr. Kevin McCauley and Dr. Cory Reich in early 2007. They are two doctors who work with addicts and advocate and use the latest research on addiction.

My wife Marie and I originally wrote down these questions as we were experiencing the helpless and hopeless feelings that come with having a loved one with addiction. We had struggled with our son Mike and were desperately trying to help him. We know about the overwhelming need to try to find answers to questions: Why were our attempts to help our son failing? Was this our fault? What is addiction? Is it really a disease? Where can we turn for help? Does spirituality work?

Finding answers to these questions and others does bring relief and hope. It was not until we sat down with Dr. McCauley and Dr. Reich, and they explained the new research about addiction, that we began to understand that this was not our fault, and that addiction was a brain disease that can be successfully treated.

Sadly, this information reached our family too late to help our son Mike. With much sorrow and pain, Marie and I have buried our son. We have endured our loss of Mike through our faith and have been blessed by the tender mercies of the Savior.

From our great loss has come a deep desire and determination to help other families find the answers they seek from the fragile world of addiction. That is why we put this book together. We hope that it will explain addiction, what it is, and what can be done about it. We believe this information can save lives. We believe it will bring real hope, optimism, and even peace.

We did this for our family and yours.

But most of all, we did it for Mike!

Marie and Jim Clegg

Chapter One: Addiction: Is it Really a "Disease?"

This book is about addiction. Specifically, it is about why addiction is a disease, and how it can be treated effectively.

Calling addiction a disease might offend you, especially if you are—right now—trying to cope with an addicted family member. If so, you know the pain an addict brings into a family, even when you try everything to reach them. Addicts steal money from their parents. They lie, or are unfaithful to their spouses. They bitterly disappoint their children. They disappear for long periods of time, leaving their loved ones to worry what crisis will befall them next.

We won't deny that addicts do terrible things. So how can addiction be a "disease?" Isn't calling addiction a "disease" just an excuse for bad behavior? And why should we recommend "treatment" for the addict, when perhaps what we really want to do is kick them out of the house, or fire them from their job, or throw them in jail. Nothing else works!

It is not our intent to offend you—or confuse or frustrate you—by using words like "disease" and "treatment" in the same breath as "addict." Far from it—because we work with addicts every day, we understand very well the pain you and your family go through.

But along with your anger and frustration and hurt, we believe that you also remember a time when your addicted family member did not act this way. We're guessing that you remember a different person—loving, decent, trustworthy. A good child. A devoted spouse. A best friend.

That memory is what we're trying to appeal to in writing this book—that deep down you know that there is more to your addicted loved one than just their bad behavior, that there might be an explanation for why they do the things they do.

Well the truth is: you're right!

Addicts do terrible things—they lie, they cheat, and they steal. But it turns out that they are not inherently liars, cheats or thieves. There are, in fact, very good reasons—*brain chemistry reasons*—for the things that addicts do. Writing the addict off as just a bad person is too quick, too easy. There is a disease process behind those behaviors, and that disease process is called addiction, and that is what we will talk about in this book.

If all we do is look at the addict's behavior, we will quickly form some strong opinions about who they are as a person. We can't help it; their behavior is just too shocking. We will make confident pronouncements about their character, their friends, perhaps even their upbringing. And we may use certain phrases to describe addicts, like "addicts are morally weak." Or "alcoholics have an addictive personality." Sometimes even addicts use these terms to describe themselves: "Watch out! I'm an addict: I will lie and manipulate to get what I want!"

These commonly-held beliefs about addicts are very powerful. They make sense. We take them at face value.

But we would like to ask an odd question.

What if we're wrong?

What if these commonly-held beliefs about the nature of addicts—assured as they may seem—are just plain wrong?

How could we even suggest such a thing? Have we lost our minds? No. We want to point out that we have made this mistake before.

Sometimes, when the behavior of patients is particularly disturbing, and the medical or psychological cause of that behavior is not immediately apparent, we can fall back on explanations that blame the behavior on the patient's upbringing or social group, or their moral or personality flaws. These attitudes toward certain groups of people are judgmental and highly prejudicial. They are stereotypes, really—and throughout the history of medicine and psychology there are many examples of intelligent and well-meaning doctors who fell into this trap. It was not that long ago that psychiatrists and psychologists thought that women were prone to hysteria because of their inherent "feminine nature." Or that African-Americans were more likely to have sexually transmitted diseases because of their intrinsic moral turpitude. At the turn of the last century, some Public Health officials in New York and Boston believed that Irish Catholics were especially susceptible to cholera because of their religious and cultural practices. Often these stereotypes led doctors to recommend shockingly abusive treatments for their patients.

Fortunately, no one believes these things anymore. In each case, scientists learned something new about the way the brain or the body works that revealed the true cause of these behaviors. Slowly and painfully, doctors and psychologists learned that moral character, social environment, gender, race and religion were not the reasons behind these behaviors. They were, in fact, *symptoms*—of a *disease* process. This new understanding led to more effective treatment. But when thinking about addiction, we must keep in mind this long and unfortunate history in medicine and psychology of characterizing people whose behavior we didn't much like and little understood in terms of their morals, their personality, their gender, race, or creed. Time and time again these characterizations have been wrong. How do we know we're not making the same mistake again—with addicts?

In fact, there is no such thing as an "addict personality." Five decades of clinical research has never been able to identify a particular kind of personality or unique set of character traits that go along with addiction. Likewise, addiction occurs in people regardless of their upbringing and social environment. While moral flaws, character defects and family dysfunction can indeed *accompany* addiction, they cannot, in fact, cause addiction. Something else causes addiction— and in this book we will discuss that cause and how best to treat it. We have learned something new about the way the brain works that paints a different picture of addiction—as a brain disease—and recent advances in neuroscience make us realize that many of our commonly held beliefs about addicts are simply wrong.

For the first time in the history of medicine, doctors have some hard and fast facts about what happens to the human brain when it becomes addicted to drugs and alcohol. And this new neuroscientific understanding of addiction is very exciting, because it gives powerful new tools to parents and siblings, spouses and friends, employers and therapists to help the addict enter treatment and rebuild their life.

If your family has a loved one who is struggling with addiction, or if you have a close friend or employee who is using drugs or alcohol, you are not alone. Research shows that addiction impacts the lives of one in five people. Our goal in writing this book is to introduce you to this new information about addiction—to explain what addiction is, and what happens in the brain of an addict when they use drugs or alcohol. We assume that if you are reading this book, addiction has touched you or your family, and you need some answers and tools to cope—now!

We want to provide those answers.

We want you to have those tools.

We will try to help you make some sense of your addict's behavior. And we will do our best to show you that, when it comes to addiction, *there is hope*.

We read the new research about addiction as it is published in medical journals. Each month, even more information about addiction comes out! And as we read these journals, one thought rises to the surface in our minds: the news about addiction treatment is good. In fact, there has never been a better time for a person who wants recovery to get sober. Each year we understand addiction better. Now there are some new medications to help people get through their first year of sobriety—powerfully effective medications that weren't available just a few years ago. More people come to treatment earlier in the course of their addiction, and they achieve sobriety in their first or second attempts at treatment—not their eighth or ninth or tenth. There is every reason to be optimistic that your addict can be treated, that he or she can regain a hold on life and repair the damage caused by their addiction, and that your family can begin a healing process that will, in the long run, make it stronger than ever.

There is one point we wish to make abundantly clear: we do not believe that any of this new research excuses bad behavior, or absolves the addict of the responsibility to account for the pain they may have caused those around them. We understand how some may think we are doing that when we call addiction a disease, or advocate for its treatment as a medical problem. But we believe that both of the following statements are true: Addiction is a disease, *and* addicts must take responsibility for managing it.

Now we will admit: there is something irritating about calling an addict a "patient" with a "disease" in the same way that we might think of a diabetic or a person with cancer as a "patient" with a "disease." Addicts, after all, *choose* to use drugs. A diabetic does not *choose* to get diabetes. Cancer *befalls* an unfortunate person. Addicts do it to *themselves*.

These are very good arguments against the conceptualization of addiction as a "disease." They are part of what we call the "Choice Argument." The Choice Argument is the opponent of the "Disease Argument." It says that addiction cannot be a disease because drug taking is a *behavior* and all behaviors are *choices*. Real diseases do not involve choice. Diabetics cannot choose to have a low blood sugar. But addicts can choose to stop using drugs. The addict might tell you that they can't help themselves—that they are *powerless* over drugs and alcohol—but really they can stop anytime they want. This is the Choice Argument, and as a demonstration of its point the Choice Argument suggests that if you offer drugs or alcohol to an addict, but put a gun to their head and tell them that if they use they will be shot, the addict will choose not to use. This is not a possibility for the diabetic. A gun to the head will not help them choose to lower their blood sugar. Diabetes is a real disease. Addiction is a choice.

We have tremendous respect for the Choice Argument. We study its propositions and challenges carefully.

But we still feel that it is wrong.

We feel the Choice Argument is wrong because it misses a fundamental point about addiction. When a drug or alcohol is offered to an addict while a gun points at their head as a threatened consequence of use, it is true that the addict can choose not to use or drink. But that is not the end of the story. Even though the addict is not using, they still *crave* drugs.

Craving is an intense, emotional, obsessive thought process that occurs in addicts. It does not occur in non-addicts, or even in bad abusers. It is a form of neural activity that is visible on sophisticated brain scans. For the addict, it is true suffering.

And, most importantly, it is *involuntary*.

Craving is a fundamental aspect, perhaps the most fundamental aspect, of addiction. It is not possible to understand addiction without taking the phenomenon of craving into account, and how it impairs the addict's ability to exercise choice.

Addiction, it turns out, is a disorder of *volition*. It is a broken "choice" system in the brain. One of the most exciting aspects of this new research in neuroscience is that it reveals to us how "choice" actually works. And addicts, through their suffering, give us the opportunity to study how our capacity to exercise choice goes wrong.

We plan to explain these advances in greater detail ahead, but for now it is important to understand that poor choice can be part of a disease process. There are mechanisms in the brain of an addict that cause free will to fail. There are even factors at work in our lives—some of them genetic—that influence our decision to take the first drink, or use the first drug. It turns out these things are not always in our control, and yet they play a big part in determining a person's vulnerability to addiction.

One thing we should point out as we try to unravel the "Choice vs. Disease" debate: part of our difficulty in calling addiction a disease, and our concern that if addiction is a disease that it may be difficult to hold anyone accountable for their behavior (they could just claim that they have a "disease"), stems from the way our modern concept of "disease" evolved.

Our modern definition of disease, what we will call the Disease Model, emerged from Germ Theory about a hundred years ago—from the work of early microbiologists, such as Louis Pasteur. The Disease Model says that a "disease" is some physical, cellular *defect* that occurs in an *organ* in the body that leads to *symptoms*.

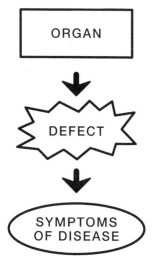

Figure 1. *The Disease Model*

We feel that is a very good definition of "disease" because it captures how doctors use the concept in medicine today. They try to treat a patient's symptoms by knowing the defect in an organ and fixing it. Nearly a century ago, doctors designed the modern practice of medicine around this new definition of "disease."

From its inception, the Disease Model was a powerful model. It helped doctors discover the causes of many previously misunderstood diseases. It curtailed the practice of attributing patients' symptoms to their gender or race or personality or social environment. Most importantly, the Disease Model saved millions—perhaps billions—of lives. It solved a lot of problems in medicine, this Disease Model. But it created others.

The Disease Model—good as it is—suffers from the fact that it is a purely *material* model. It deals with physical things: molecules, membranes, *matter*. As such, it forces two kinds of solutions to medical and psychological problems: pills, and surgeries. It does not address the *meaning* that illness can have for patients. This is why doctors are very good at performing stomach-stapling operations for obese patients, but they are quite poor at understanding what food *means* to such patients. Likewise, the Disease Model cannot explain what occurs when a person has a spiritual experience. It has a hard time addressing the healing power of faith.

The human brain is a very special organ. It does more than just take in sensory data and process motor commands. It makes *meaning*. We all *make meaning*. In fact, beyond our basic instinct to survive, we humans have an inherent drive to create meaning in our lives. This capacity to create *meaning* is fundamental to our capacity to exert *choice*. This is why meaning and the capacity to exercise choice are both so important to the healing of the disease of addiction.

But perhaps the most disturbing problem with the Disease Model—and the problem that causes so much of the strife surrounding the "Choice vs. Disease" debate—is that the Disease Model tends to strip patients of their power to make their own decisions regarding their health. The Disease Model then hands that power to the doctor. As compensation for this exchange of power, the patient is encouraged to enter the "sick role"—which is a compliant role, a helpless role, and a role relieved of responsibility.

In the kind of medicine the Disease Model gives us, the doctor does all the work to get the patient healthy. The patient is not held accountable for their own wellness.

We feel that most of the difficulty people have in calling addiction a "disease" stems not from whether or not addiction fits our modern definition of "disease" (because it does). Our difficulty arises from the problems inherent in the Disease Model itself. And one of our goals in writing this book is to try to put *meaning* and *spirituality* and *accountability* back into our definition of disease. Without these things, we believe treatment for addiction will fail.

But with them, the addict will not just live, but thrive—and the family cannot help but heal.

Chapter Two: Addiction, Stress and Dopamine

Is addiction really a "disease"?

We feel that this is the most important question there is about addiction. All the other questions about addiction, whether they are medical, psychological, legal, political, or historical, really start with this question: with addiction, are we even dealing with a bona-fide disease process? In many ways, we cannot have an intelligent discussion about addiction until we get the answer to this question right. So this is where we must begin.

Fortunately, we have a good definition of disease.

A disease is a defect in an organ that leads to symptoms.

This modern concept of disease is almost a century old. In that time it proved very successful at helping doctors treat sick patients. It is easy to see how diabetes or a broken leg can fit that model (See Fig 2). The causes of these diseases are fairly straightforward. They take place in organs that are relatively easy to study—the pancreas, and bone. And the treatments for these diseases—set the bone, replace the insulin—present themselves readily. But while broken legs and diabetes fit the Disease Model easily, addiction does not. Addiction is not as straightforward. Its cause is complex. And the organ involved—the brain—is difficult to study. One hundred years ago, doctors chose the Disease Model as their new, modern, scientific definition of human illness, and while they could readily fit many simple diseases to that model, they could not fit addiction to the Disease Model. They declared that it wasn't a disease at all. Diabetics and patients with broken legs received medical care. But addiction was no longer considered a disease. Addicts were left to fend for themselves.

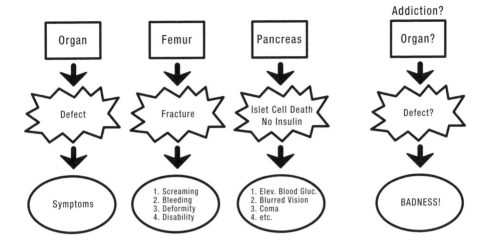

Figure 2. Diseases that fit and Diseases that do not fit the Disease Model

But now we finally can fit addiction to this definition of disease. With the new neuroscientific understanding of addiction, now we can say, "Addiction is a disease" and actually prove it.

So let's do that—let's fit addiction to the "Disease Model."

The organ involved in addiction is the brain, or more accurately the *Midbrain*. The Midbrain is the part of the brain that handles our most basic survival drives. Our emotional responses begin in the Midbrain. It is not conscious. It doesn't think, so it doesn't deliberate over decisions of what to do, nor does it weigh moral consequences. The Midbrain simply acts to save the organism's life. It is the automatic, here-and-now, eat-kill-sex, do-whatever-it-takes-to-survive part of the brain.

The job of keeping the Midbrain in check falls to the Frontal Cortex. This is the conscious, thinking, deliberating, moral part of the brain. The Frontal Cortex exercises good judgment. It is the part of the brain where we attach—this is where we love our parents, our children, our spouses, our friends. The Frontal

Cortex is also the part of the brain where we construct our personality, and have a social life. Most importantly, this is the part of the brain where we give the concepts and objects that enter our world their meaning. This, then, makes the Frontal Cortex the spiritual part of the brain.

In a healthy brain, the Frontal Cortex exerts a kind of "top-down" control over the Midbrain. When we make choices, the things that are meaningful to us are stronger in guiding our behavior than our basic survival drives. But in addiction, something goes wrong in the Midbrain such that this "top-down" control fails, and the Midbrain becomes more powerful than the Frontal Cortex. The survival drives win out—even over the things that used to be deeply, emotionally—even spiritually—meaningful to us. This can lead to some shocking behaviors indeed—behaviors that look like badness. But these behaviors are not badness. Upsetting as they are, these are the symptoms of addiction.

In addiction, the organ involved is the Midbrain. Something goes wrong at a level of brain processing prior to that of the frontal cortex, and at a level of brain processing that takes place long before morals or love or thinking or spirituality.

So now we can fill in the organ part of the Disease Model: the organ is the Midbrain. What about the defect—the actual cause of addiction?

A lot of attention has been given to the genetic aspect of addiction. Well, it's true that genes are very important in addiction. But we must be careful not to think that genes are the sole cause of addiction, because they are not. How do we know this? Because there are lots of people with a strong family history of addiction—they have parents and grandparents with alcoholism, they have siblings with addiction—and yet they don't become alcoholics or addicts. Likewise, there are lots of people with no family history of addiction—no alcoholics or addicts anywhere in their family—and yet they still become addicts. What does this tell us? This tells us that genes can predispose a person for addiction; they are a *necessary* cause for addiction. But they are not *a necessary and sufficient* cause for addiction.

There is no "alcoholism gene" or "addict gene" for the simple reason that a single defective gene cannot cause a disease as complex as addiction. Not even two or three defective genes can cause addiction. Addiction is probably caused by many different genes—perhaps as many as two or three-dozen genes, some defective, some normal—interacting with the environment in such a way as to cause the expression of the disease. Blaming addiction on the genes that the addict inherited from his or her mother or father is inaccurate. For addiction to develop, we need something that acts on the genes to produce addiction—something in the environment that is the necessary *and* sufficient cause of addiction.

So what is that thing in the environment that turns on the genes that lead to (causes?) addiction? It's *stress*. Addiction is a stress-induced defect deep in the midbrain.

This answer may be difficult to accept—after all, we all face stress, but we don't all smoke crack cocaine. This is true. But the kind of stress that we're talking about here is *severe* stress. The person has lived through some trauma. Or perhaps suffers from an undiagnosed mental illness. Or they have endured a slow but steady and increasingly severe level of stress over time. Sometimes drug use itself can cause enough stress to produce the defect in the midbrain that leads to addiction. These stressors, if they are severe enough, persist long enough, and are not resolved, can cause chronically elevated levels of stress hormones—the most important of which is called Corticotropin-Releasing Factor, or CRF. This CRF sensitizes the stress system in the Midbrain. Eventually, the Midbrain interprets this stress not just as unpleasant, but as an actual threat to survival. Severe stress *changes* the midbrain. Chronic, severe stress *breaks* the midbrain. And specifically what breaks in the midbrain is the Dopamine system.

The Dopamine system in the brain does many things, but what matters for our discussion is that Dopamine is the chemical the brain uses to give us the feeling of *pleasure*. Our brain uses pleasure to identify things in the environment that have survival value. If a person is starving, chocolate cake is more likely to save their life than broccoli. This is why chocolate cake tastes better than broccoli: it releases more dopamine. That Dopamine, in turn, relieves the survival stressor of hunger. So in our brains we have a perceptual mechanism that can identify things that have high survival value—our "pleasure sense." Neuroscientists have a more technical term for the brain's pleasure sense. They call it the brain's "hedonic capacity." The two are essentially the same thing. The bottom line is this: we can tell the difference between broccoli and chocolate cake.

High levels of stress—and thus high levels of that hormone CRF—cause the Dopamine system to fail. The "pleasure sense" breaks. Normal pleasures—and thus normal releases of dopamine—are not enough for the stressed person to feel pleasure. There is no relief of stress. Chronic, severe stress causes the person's midbrain to become *anhedonic*—their midbrain can no longer derive normal pleasure from normally pleasurable things. These people are, in a very real sense, pleasure *deaf*. If you take one of these stressed and anhedonic people to Disneyland, they don't enjoy it. Everyone around them at Disneyland is having a good time. They don't get it. And they may have enjoyed Disneyland in the past. But now their world goes grey. Normal pleasures—normal releases of Dopamine—do not register in their brains.

The defect in addiction is a stress-induced dysregulation of the brain's hedonic system—its "pleasure sense."

So what does register? What can the now "deaf" pleasure sense "hear?" Anything that...well, *shouts*! Anything that produces *big* surges of Dopamine. The stressed and anhedonic person will be able to "hear" that. And what causes big surges of Dopamine in the brain?

Drugs.

All drugs—whether they are uppers or downers, or strong or weak, or legal or illegal—have one common feature: they can produce large surges of Dopamine in the midbrain.

And what are the chemicals that produce these large surges of Dopamine? Here they are:

Sedative/Hypnotics

These are drugs that decrease anxiety and promote sleep. Examples include alcohol, barbiturates, benzodiazepines, and sleep aids such as zolpidem (Ambien) and zaleplon (Sonata). GHB is also considered a sedative/hypnotic.

Opiates and Opioids

These are the classic "narcotics"—powerful analgesics (pain relievers) that have a high potential for abuse. Examples include codeine, morphine, hydrocodone (Vicodin and Lortab), methadone and heroin.

Cocaine

A major stimulant.

Amphetamines

Also major stimulants. This is a large class of drugs that includes many prescription stimulants such as methylphenidate (Ritalin) as well crystal methamphetamine (also known as "Ice" or "Crank").

Entactogens

Drugs that generate novel tactile experiences. Examples include MDA and MDMA ("Ecstasy").

Entheogens

Drugs that generate novel mystical or spiritual experiences. Examples include LSD, mescaline, psilocybin and psychedelic mushrooms.

Dissociants

These drugs produce a depersonalized or "out of body" feeling. Examples include PCP (aka Angel Dust), Ketamine (aka Special K), and large doses of Dextromethorphan (Robotussin).

Cannabinoids

The class of psychoactive chemicals found in marijuana.

Inhalants

Organic solvents used in "huffing." Also includes nitrous oxide.

Nicotine

A minor stimulant.

Caffeine

Also a minor stimulant.

Anabolic-Androgenic Steroids

Drugs that increase muscle mass and male sex characteristics (not the same as catabolic steroids such as Prednisone).

Whether they are uppers or downers, strong or weak, legal or illegal, all of these drugs have one feature in common: they can cause surges of dopamine in the midbrain. (The last sentence repeats what was already stated, is this done for emphasis? If so, we may want to begin the sentence with—Again,...) So if a person has an addiction to one, they have a liability for the others. This is why the alcoholic cannot stop drinking by moving to marijuana. The person has not learned to deal with their stress and eventually the dopamine surge caused by the marijuana will re-ignite their cravings for alcohol. This is why cocaine and methamphetamine addicts who continue to chain smoke and drink large amounts of caffeinated beverages will notice their cravings get worse. They are still releasing dopamine in the midbrain. If they are not careful, the cigarettes and coffee may cause them to relapse back to cocaine or methamphetamine.

But not only drugs can cause causes big surges of Dopamine in the Midbrain. Addicts do other things to release Dopamine to cope with stress. These things can also become addictions in their own right, or they can accompany the use of the chemical and worsen craving. What are these other things that release Dopamine?

Behaviors:

Food

Addiction to food expresses itself as Bulimia and Binge-eating disorders.

Sex

Relationships

Other People

This addiction is more commonly referred to as "Codependency."

Gambling

Cults

Performance

These are addictions such as "work-aholism" and over-exercise.

Collection and Accumulation

This includes "shop-aholism" and compulsive spending.

Rage and Violence

This is a dangerous addiction in which the person learns to manipulate their anger to release inappropriate surges of Dopamine.

Media

Examples include internet and video game addiction.

It is important to recognize that the addict is not performing these behaviors for their intrinsic enjoyment. The addict is manipulating a pleasurable experience to cope with stress—to get that Dopamine surge and decrease those high levels of CRF. The midbrain recognizes this stress relief. In fact, it notices that the drug is the best stress reliever it has ever come across. So the drug now becomes the midbrain's number one way of securing survival. The drug trumps all other survival behaviors—it is stronger than the urge to eat, stronger than the urge to kill or defend oneself, stronger than the urge for sex. For this midbrain, the drug is so close to actual survival that now the drug and survival are one and the same. The drug has been tagged by the midbrain with survival salience. Now anytime the addict becomes stressed, the midbrain goes straight to the thing that it knows is best at relieving that stress quickly: the drug. Or the behavior. Or both. For the addict, the drug simply *is* survival.

Very often, the addict will succeed in decreasing their drinking or drug use only to increase their behavioral addiction. The classic example is the cocaine addict who stops cocaine, but whose sexual acting out—with prostitutes, affairs or pornography—increases correspondingly. Unfortunately, these behaviors cause surges of Dopamine, and they in turn worsen the addict's craving for their drug. This quickly leads the addict to relapse back to the drug.

One interesting item on this list—and of particular application to families coping with an addicted loved-one—is "Codependency."

Early on in the treatment of addicts it was noticed that alcoholics almost always seem to have another person in their life who, in subtle ways, enables their drinking.

This person was labeled the "co-alcoholic." That term proved too upsetting to family members who visited treatment centers to participate in the alcoholic's treatment, so the term was changed to "co-dependent." The co-dependent does not think they are hurting the alcoholic, but the interaction between the two makes it difficult for the addictive behavior to stop. The co-dependent person is obsessed with the behavior of the addict and they feel compelled to control the behavior of the addict. Usually they do not succeed in controlling the addict. But every now and then their controlling behavior does work, and they get a little surge of dopamine. So co-dependency can be like a little mini-addiction. That's why treatment centers recommend that the family members of addicts in treatment go to Al-Anon. There they can start to see how their enabling behavior is making their life unmanageable and they can begin the process to learn how to stop them.

Since this connection of the drug to survival occurs very deep in the brain and at a very early level of brain processing, when the addict becomes stressed the urge to use drugs begins before the addict is even aware of it. Emotional or sensory experiences can start this process. Even places that the addict used drugs in the past can create the urge to use drugs. These are what are known as "triggers," and they can result in relapse to drugs or alcohol. One of the main tasks of treatment is to teach the addict how to avoid these triggers and how to manage their stress in such a way as to avoid relapse.

But there is something that can complicate this process. When the midbrain is stressed, it has two rather cruel tools at its disposal to ensure that the addict continues using the drug.

One tool is called craving, and as we said earlier craving is an intense, emotional urge to use the drug. It is an obsession—in fact, on brain scans the same areas of the brain that are active in obsessive-compulsive disorder are active in the addict's brain during craving. No matter how hard the addict tries to think of other things, the stressed midbrain returns the addicts thoughts to the drug. Drug use, for the addict, is no longer about a party. It is about life itself.

The second tool the midbrain has is "denial." You may have heard of this term—it describes the addict's refusal to recognize just how bad their drug use or drinking is. They normalize. They deflect blame. They won't believe what others can clearly see. The midbrain uses denial to protect its access to the one thing it knows can get it through the next thirty seconds of life: the drug.

We understand the power of the word denial to describe a very real phenomenon that occurs in addicts. But we are concerned that denial is an indefensible hypothesis: any evidence the addict offers that they are not in denial is further evidence that they are in denial. This circular logic can be frustrating for therapist, family and addict alike. We recognize that denial exists, but we think neuroscientists have a better term for it: frontal hypofunctionality. This is a large word for the fact that, during craving, the frontal cortex of the addict simply shuts off. For the midbrain the addict's morals, emotional connections to their family and friends are now liabilities. They stand in the way of survival. So the midbrain simply shuts the cortex down. The normal "top-down" control of the frontal cortex over the midbrain reverses. The midbrain is now in charge.

This process is actually visible on a new kind of brain scan called a "functional MRI." When an addict is placed in the fMRI machine and shown pictures of people using drugs, they begin to crave. Their midbrain lights up like a Christmas tree. Their frontal cortex goes dark. The part of their brain that says, "I don't want to do this. Remember how bad it was last time? I don't want to go back to jail. I don't want to hurt my family" is simply off.

The behavior exhibited by the addict during frontal hypofunctionality is not pleasant. The addict will lie in the service of their craving midbrain to get drugs. They will steal to get drugs. They will manipulate and cheat. It may look like the addict doesn't have any values and morals—that they are in fact a liar, cheat, and a thief. But that's not actually what's going on. In the heat of stress and craving, the addict cannot draw on their values or morals or willpower to guide their behavior. The midbrain thinks that this is about life and death, and it will do whatever is necessary and will mobilize everything at its disposal to secure survival—to get and use drugs.

This behavior isn't pretty, but it's not quite the same thing as badness.

This is why addiction may look like sociopathy, but it is not the same thing. The sociopath has no remorse. They have no ability to empathize with another person. When they are beating someone, they do not understand that other people feel pain the way they feel pain. When they are stealing something, they do not grasp that other people have property rights the way they do. Sociopaths do not have a disease. They do not respond to treatment. They really are bad people. (I believe we just remove these last three sentences, the point of distinction is relevant, yet I believe we are talking about a different type of disease process in sociopaths not just a "bad" person, I would hate to open a distracting debate.)

Addicts are not sociopaths. When they use drugs and bad things happen, they feel bad. They are racked with remorse over the things they have done.

They feel terrible about the people they have hurt. But because they cannot tolerate bad feelings (the midbrain interprets them as a survival threat), they must do something to escape those bad feelings—so they use drugs, and the cycle repeats. This "addict cycle" is driven by shame, guilt, and remorse—exactly the things you don't see in the sociopath.

And unlike sociopaths, if addicts get into recovery, if they stop using drugs and learn to manage stress, and decrease their craving, then all of that lying, cheating, stealing goes away. Their frontal cortex comes back online. And then the real person—the son or the daughter or the friend or the employee or the mom or the dad that we all remember comes right back.

So now we have a working definition of addiction:

Addiction is a stress-induced defect in the midbrain's dopamine system—its hedonic system—resulting in symptoms of decreased functioning, namely:

1. Loss of Control

2. Craving, and

3. Persistent Use of the Drug/Behavior Despite Negative Consequences

Please take note of the third symptom, because this is the one that causes all the problems. It would stand to reason that if the addict were faced with prison or the loss of their child that they would stop using. We deal with a lot of addicts, and that is exactly what we do not see. If we threaten the addict to motivate them to enter or stay in treatment, what we see is that their drug use *accelerates*. Why? Because we are stressing the addict before they have the tools in place to manage that stress. We have noticed that if we are not careful, we can actually *induce* relapse in the patient.

So now we can fit addiction to the Disease Model:

Figure 3. Addiction Fits the Disease Model

We began our inquiry into the question of whether or not addiction was really a "disease" by coming up with a very tough definition of "disease." This definition is so tough that many conditions that are considered diseases without contest would have a hard time meeting this standard. But now we can fit addiction to this definition—better than we can many "diseases!" This is why we can—with confidence—say that addiction really, truly is a **disease**.

Chapter Three: Helping the Addict Accept Treatment

You may have heard the saying that "you can't help an addict if they don't want help."

Or perhaps you've heard that "the addict has to be ready to stop using drugs and alcohol before they can begin treatment."

Here's one that never fails to provoke anxiety in family members: "the addict has to hit bottom before they can get sober."

These statements—often spoken with confidence by people working in the addiction treatment field—can frighten any family struggling with a loved-one addicted to drugs or alcohol. This is especially true for the "hit bottom" statement because it begs the next question: what will your addict's bottom be? An overdose? Jail? Worse? The statement seems to invite disaster.

It's always nice if the patient comes to treatment and says, "I've had enough—I'm ready to quit." But even if the patient says, "Drugs and alcohol are the best thing that's ever happened to me—I'm never going to quit," a good therapist or treatment center can work with this patient, too. There are things that can be done to help the addict increase their willingness to change and commit to quit. Asking the patient to come to treatment ready to quit is tantamount to asking the patient to come to treatment already *half-treated*. Every addict wants help. They may not admit it, they may not want help today, or they may want the wrong kind of help—but they do want help. If we offer the right help at the right time, we can raise the addict's "bottom" to a level that won't leave them with tragic, life-long and irreparable damage.

This kind of therapy looks very different from older methods that were much more confrontational and coercive. It is more effective because it compliments the process that people undergo as they decide to change their unhealthy behaviors.

Ambivalence

One of the more interesting features of the human brain is its ability to hold two ideas—sometimes two directly opposite and mutually exclusive ideas—in the mind at the same time. We may complain about our job and long for retirement, but can't tear ourselves away even for a short vacation. We may love a person deeply, but also hate them for the things they do to us. The addict's mind is no different: two strong but incompatible ideas are present at once.

Let's take smoking. The smoker likes to smoke, and they have decided that they are going to keep on smoking cigarettes. Their decision on the matter is firm and not open to discussion. But perhaps they're starting to notice some problems caused by smoking cigarettes. The morning cough. The arguments with the family. Having to stand outside in the cold to smoke at work. The smoker hates this part of smoking. They really would like to quit. Basically, what the smoker is trying to do is find a way to stop smoking cigarettes...without having to actually stop smoking cigarettes. This may sound crazy, but it is a mental conflict that every addict recognizes. In fact, addicts go through this "back-and-forth" process all day long.

This inner conflict is called *ambivalence*. It's like a little mental seesaw that tips back and forth. Most of the time "keep on using drugs" is stronger. But occasionally "stop using drugs" gets the upper hand—if only briefly.

A good therapist knows how to work with this ambivalence. They can employ therapeutic techniques that help the addict stack more weight on the "stop using drugs" side. Quitting drugs begins to have more value for the addict than continuing to use drugs. Over time the addict's willingness to leave drugs behind increases. This increase in the addict's internal motivation to quit is especially likely if they feel like they're understood and accepted by their therapist.

It's important to keep in mind that, for the smoker, cigarettes have real meaning. But during the process of change, other things—things not compatible with smoking—become more meaningful. One of the most powerful tools a doctor or therapist can use to help a person quit smoking is the statement, "Hey, I know you love cigarettes—but don't you want to make sure you can dance at your granddaughter's wedding?" Poof! The smoker quits. Well, it's not quite that quick—there are a few relapses. But a good therapist knows to stay with the patient as this process of change unfolds—to see them through cravings and motivational setbacks—until they eventually come around to wanting to try to quit in earnest. And then they do.

You may have also heard the saying "addicts never seek help on their own." That's not quite true. There are plenty of examples of addicts seeking help on their own. In addiction medicine, there is almost forty years of success using Employee Assistance Programs to identify, intervene and treat addiction in the workplace. When these programs are run well, very often workers with drug and alcohol problems *do* seek help on their own. Traditionally, these programs provide workers in safety-sensitive jobs with the ability to self-report their drug or alcohol problem and get treatment with the knowledge that they won't lose their jobs. After treatment, they can go back to work—provided they agree to have their recovery monitored. What is important about these programs is that they deliberately frame addiction as a safety issue, not a moral issue. And these employees know that their self-disclosure will be met with understanding and support, not with judgment and punishment. The experience of these programs is that workers come forward at an earlier stage of their addiction, when it is easier to treat. So people can seek help on their own for drug and alcohol problems—if we provide the right kind of support for them to do so. We will talk more about one of these groups of workers who come to treatment on their own a bit later.

Withdrawal and Detoxification

When a person first comes to treatment, the first step is to provide them with a good detoxification.

The importance of detox cannot be overstated. During withdrawal from drugs such as alcohol or opioids, the brain is in a hyper excited state. That hyper excited state is toxic to the brain. Delirium tremens—the symptoms of agitation, psychosis and seizures that accompany sudden alcohol cessation in an alcohol-tolerant patient—can have as high as a twenty percent mortality rate if left untreated. Severe withdrawal is a medical emergency that should be treated in a hospital.

In the past, detox was miserable. Very little was done for addicts in the throes of drug or alcohol withdrawal. A common opinion held that the addict should suffer during detox, because it would make them think twice about relapsing. Many heroin addicts could not make it through the detox process. Their withdrawal symptoms were too painful, and they went back to heroin for relief. Alcoholics checked themselves out of treatment because their anxiety and cravings were overwhelming. Many addicts came to treatment, only to be lost in the middle of a bad detox.

In fact, research shows no connection between the pain of detox and the length of time an addict remains abstinent. There is however a strong connection between providing the patient a comfortable, medically-assisted detoxification and treatment success in the first year of recovery. This is why detox is so important: it sets the stage for everything to come in treatment and the first year of recovery. Cold-turkey detox is not only ineffective, it is inhumane.

Today, doctors have several new medications that can provide the addict with a comfortable, safe, and most importantly successful detoxification. They stop the pain of withdrawal for the addict. They can ease cravings in the alcoholic. These medications cushion the brain through this dangerous period. A comfortable detox makes it more likely that the patient will stay in treatment, and remain sober afterward.

Detox is also a good opportunity to *care* for the patient—to sit with them, talk with them, rest a hand on their wrist, stay with them through the pain of withdrawal. Most patients respond quite well to this kind of care. Addicts do too. This is the best time for the patient and therapist or doctor to build a relationship of trust. This will be important later, when the therapist or doctor has to tell the addict things they may not want to hear. Once the two are working from a relationship grounded in compassion, the addict is more likely to perceive the therapist's confrontation and direction as genuine concern, not criticism. This will make all the difference as the two negotiate the rocky terrain of change.

Craving

Almost every addict who comes to treatment has tried to quit on his or her own. They try mightily. They are certain they can do it. They make sincere promises to themselves and others that they will stop. Unfortunately, it doesn't work. Once they get stressed, their frontal cortex shuts down and the midbrain takes over. Their conscious appreciation of the needs of their loved ones, or of dire consequences—jail, loss of job—should they relapse, are a dim memory. Now the midbrain governs their choices. Consciousness constricts. Choice fails. But that stress—perceived by the midbrain as a survival threat—demands relief. And to motivate the individual to relieve that stress, the midbrain initiates craving. Never forget: for the addict, craving is no joke!

Craving is an intense emotional longing for the drug. Most importantly, craving is *involuntary*. The addict does not choose to crave, nor can the addict willfully turn off their craving. No amount of threats will break through that craving because the midbrain equates the drug with *survival*. Nothing is a greater priority than survival. The midbrain must secure survival at all costs. So the drug comes first. Everything else is second.

This is craving. And make no mistake: it is genuine *suffering*.

It is only when the addict comes to treatment and learns about the connection between their stress, their drug and their craving that they begin to see how to stop this relapse reflex. They learn the importance of good, pro-active stress management. This knowledge does not come immediately. Sometimes, it takes the addict several tries. But most people who persevere eventually succeed. As they learn the skills of recovery, the relapses eventually stop.

With time, the addict's "pleasure sense" comes back to normal. The addict is no longer anhedonic—or pleasure "deaf." Now they can derive normal pleasure from normally pleasurable things. At the same time, the normal function of their frontal cortex returns. Their power of choice—their capacity to exercise free will—is restored. And the person that the family remembers—their good child, their devoted spouse, their best friend—is back.

This is the person they really are!

So we must accept the fact that relapse is part of the process of recovery. That can be scary, but if we are ready for it and put enough safety nets in the addict's life—like regular post-treatment drug testing—that can catch the relapse the moment it occurs, we can prevent any terrible consequences and make it a learning process. We don't like relapse. We don't invite it. We're not happy when it happens. But it can be an opportunity to help the addict realize that if they neglect a part of their recovery plan relapse is a likely result.

Addiction and Meaning

We are often asked: If a person becomes so good at managing stress that their hedonic system is normal, can they go back to drinking? Well, theoretically this may be true. But it's not what we see clinically. Any person who is truly an addict and attempts to resume normal drinking always seems to return to an alcoholic pattern. Why might this be? We must keep in mind that, for the addict, there was at least one time when that drug or that drink worked *perfectly*. Every addict remembers that first experience—when the drug produced the dopamine surge that caused the midbrain to lock onto it as the number one stress coping tool. That memory cannot be removed. It is carved in granite, so to speak, at a very deep level of brain processing. As such, when the addict resumes drinking or drug use—even in moderation—the dopamine surge can trigger that memory and re-ignite craving. And once again, the addiction is off and running. That memory—of the one time the drug worked perfectly and the addict said, "Where has this been my whole life?"—creates a permanent liability for relapse. There is no way to erase it.

So in a sense, the addict can "manage" their stress so well that their craving is off and their addiction is quiescent—inactive, or at least temporarily dormant—and they function as normally as any other person. But there is no "cure" for addiction—not as yet. This is very similar to the way a diabetic "manages" his blood sugars and lives a normal life, but is not cured of his diabetes.

So far we have talked a lot about the brain science of addiction. This research has led to exciting new medications for addiction, and will no doubt lead to more in coming years. But even though this new neuroscientific understanding of addiction is very powerful, how is it that we know that many of the solutions that really work for addiction are of a spiritual nature? Where does faith fit into all this hard-core, materialistic brain science?

The answer presents itself if we look at addiction in two parts. The first part is that part that occurs in the midbrain: where due to a stress-induced defect in the dopamine system, the drug is misperceived, and—due to the strength of that misperception—becomes equated with survival at an unconscious level of brain processing.

What happens to that misperception? Does it just stay in the midbrain? No. It is conducted via a group of nerves known as the Median Forebrain Bundle, which travels from the midbrain to...the Frontal Cortex! That misperception of the drug's salience is delivered right to the part of the addict's brain that give the objects that enter their world their *meaning*, that allows us to *attach*, that allows us to have a *spiritual experience*. When the alcoholic says that they love alcohol—much like they would love another person—they are not lying: this is the part of the brain that allows us to love. The second part of addiction is where, for the addict, the drug takes on deep, personal meaning. The addict forms a relationship with the drug.

The task of addiction treatment is to attack both these parts of addiction at the same time. The midbrain: to give the addict tools to decrease their stress and decrease their craving. And the Frontal Cortex: to find that thing in the addict's life that is a little more emotionally meaningful than their drug. To find, as they say in Alcoholics Anonymous, their "higher power." It is this spiritual meaning that can break the hold of the drug.

So if we simply reduce addiction to the material parts of the brain, we miss something important about addiction and how to treat it. We may come up with good medications or new therapeutic techniques to reduce the symptoms of addiction, but we miss the power of spirituality to actually fix the problem.

We are excited about this new brain science of addiction, and the clinical implications of this science for the treatment of those who suffer from addiction. But we are concerned that once we've unlocked all the brain secrets of addiction, and those secrets reveal new drugs to ameliorate the symptoms of addiction, that treatment for addiction will simply devolve into the mere prescription of medications. Ultimately, this kind of treatment will fail because it leaves out the most important brain capacity of all: meaning.

Although the processes of human consciousness are realized in the substance of the brain, there is more to human consciousness than mere matter. There is a non-reducible, non-material aspect to consciousness. *We make meaning*. And the human drive to make meaning—itself a key component of our ability to exercise free will—make us spiritual beings. In addiction, all of these things—pleasure, meaning, consciousness, choice—go terribly, terribly wrong. We strongly believe that addiction is a spiritual disease, and that meaningful spiritual experiences are critical to recovery and healing. We eagerly await the many benefits that neuroscience will surely bring to relieve the suffering of addicts. But we think the revitalization of a spiritual life will always be the key to complete healing from addiction. It works in ways that traditional medicine and psychology cannot.

Chapter Four: The Problem with Punishment

Now a word about anger and punishment.

Addicts are frustrating. They put their families through much grief. It's not hard to understand why the family is angry, and why they feel if they could just get the addict's attention, perhaps break through their denial with some kind of "tough love," that their addict would snap out of it and stop their drinking and drug use.

This makes sense. But the concept of using punishment to stop addiction assumes a rational mind, and you'll remember that in addiction we are dealing with a brain disease—a true mental illness—and mental illness is under no obligation to operate according to the dictates of rationality. So appealing to the addict's reason, pleading with them, or resorting to threats of punishment will not break through the breathtaking irrationality of craving. You are trying to measure a fundamentally irrational, addicted mind with the rational yardstick that is your own, non-addicted mind. Things will not measure up. And in the end, the frustration you feel may make **you** crazy!

It is so easy to fall into this trap—the trap of trying to use punishment to get the addict to quit. But people will swear by it. They are certain that the threat of some punishment worked to get their addict to stop. Judges claim that an addict standing before him in court never would have gotten sober unless the judge had threatened him with jail. Families will say that the only way their addict would go to treatment was if they threatened to throw them out in the street. Sometimes, even addicts say these things: "I never would have quit drugs unless they had threatened to take away my little boy."

We do not claim to know what does and does not get an addict sober. Perhaps no one does in any given case. But, once again, we would like to ask a strange question.

Are we sure what's working here is the punishment?

We think not.

In our work with addicts, we have just seen too many cases where punishment did not work. We have seen addicts faced with terrible consequences if they relapsed—decades in prison, divorce, loss of their children forever—and when their craving kicked in, even those dire consequences do not keep them sober. Rewards don't seem to work either. We have seen addicts offered wonderful things—a new job, a loving marriage, an inheritance—and even these fantastic rewards did not keep the addict sober. We have even seen parents offer their son a Ferrari if he will just complete six months of treatment. It did not work.

Why doesn't punishment work? Remember: to the midbrain the drug is not just a drug—the drug is *life itself*. The drug is equated with survival at an unconscious level of brain processing. Anything the family might use to threaten the addict—divorce, arrest, loss of their children or inheritance—none of these things is more important to the midbrain than securing survival. So when craving comes on, the addict gets a message from their midbrain that goes like this: "Hey, let's just relax a minute. We're going to take care of these things. We'll get the kids back. We'll straighten everything out with the probation officer. We'll get counseling for our broken marriage. We'll do all of these things, we will…first thing tomorrow morning. Tomorrow, we'll take care of all that…but right now we're under a lot of stress, we're interpreting that stress on the level of survival, and so first we're going to secure survival—so go get that drug!" In the tragic and warped logic of craving, the addict really does believe that the best way to act responsibly and lovingly to their family is to get high right now, stay alive, and then deal with the consequences later.

This is, perhaps, the most frustrating and fascinating feature of addiction: "persistent alcohol and drug use despite negative consequences." This is one of the key diagnostic features of addiction: the addict continues to drink, continues to use drugs even when relapse may mean jail, or the loss of their family, even death. In addiction medicine, one of the ways we know we're dealing with true addiction is that punishment does not work.

So when the judge, or the family, or even the addict themselves claims that what moved the addict to get sober was a threat of punishment, what they are saying is that punishment does work.

We would like to ask: How can that be? How can the punishment not work and then work? It can't be both. There must be a confounder in there somewhere. A confounder is a fancy research term for a third variable that is actually causing the change—causing the person to snap out of it and go to treatment.

It looks like it's the punishment that gets addicts sober. We credit the punishment for breaking through the addict's denial. The addict himself may say it was the punishment. We do not think it's the punishment. If punishment worked on addiction—even if it worked just a little bit—we should see some benefit by now. The United States has incarcerated addicts for nearly a hundred years, and the problem is worse than ever. If punishment worked on addiction, our nation should have the highest addiction cure rates in the world.

So what does work? What does "snap the addict out of it"—turns their frontal cortex back on enough that it realizes just how far the midbrain has taken the addict away from their values? What finally cracks that connection of the drug to survival? Something that is deeply, personally meaningful. Something that goes to the very core of the addict's being, to their conception of self. Something that is, well...*spiritual*. These are the things that, even if just for a moment, break the hold of craving and re-establish the "top-down" control of the frontal cortex over the midbrain. The frontal cortex peeks out of its hole; consciousness clears a little. The addict suddenly sees himself as others see him. People in Alcoholics Anonymous call this a "moment of clarity." A window of opportunity has opened—but it won't be open for long! Soon the stress will return, craving will begin, and the midbrain will come roaring back to overwhelm frontal cortex and the meaningful thing will be lost again. But if we act quickly we can get the addict to treatment. There they will learn stress-coping skills they so desperately need to keep their frontal cortex not just "on" but "strong!" with their frontal cortex back on-line, the addict can again visualize a life with meaning—not the meaning that the drug had, but a meaning more in harmony with their deepest and truest values—a meaning that will once again form the backdrop of their natural exercise of their capacity of choice. From this point on—as long as they maintain their recovery on a daily basis—their spiritual life will grow and their addiction has a chance for prolonged remission.

With craving, rewards and punishments alone cannot break the drug's hold. It has to be something even more powerful than these things to the addict—something deeply, personally meaningful. It has to be something spiritual.

There is a way that the family can create such a moment—to bring the addict to the point where they can see how their alcohol and drug use has hurt the people who love them, and how far their behavior is from their values.

This is a professional intervention.

During an intervention, a therapist meets with a family and listens to how addiction has affected their lives. Sometimes the addict is present—this is called an "invitational" intervention. Sometimes the addict is not present, but the family will approach him later—this is called a "surprise" or "Johnson-style" intervention. We prefer the invitational method.

The best interventions involve the addict's entire family, their friends (who do not abuse alcohol or drugs), and sometimes even their employer and fellow employees. The intervention works best if all the people who matter to the addict are present.

The therapist/interventionist understands addiction, and is experienced in the family dynamics that go along with addiction.

The family can learn about the symptoms of addiction, and make some sense of the addict's behavior. Family members can express how their addict's behavior has affected them, and feel understood. An intervention is a confrontation, but it is not punitive. It is a loving, nonjudgmental and non-threatening offer of help.

Sometimes the addict agrees to enter treatment from the start. Sometimes they refuse. If the addict refuses help, the family then sets boundaries to protect it from further harm that the addict's drinking or drug use may cause. The family may refuse to let the addict live with them any longer. Parents may stop supporting the addict financially. The family agrees to go to Al-Anon, learn about codependency and how they unwittingly enabled the addict's continued drug use, and then the family begins to heal—even without the addict. Very often, the addict comes around and agrees to treatment.

What is happening here?

Is the addict going to treatment because of the threat of punishment? Or are they going to treatment because they are deeply moved by the fact that their family and friends came together and did everything they could to help the addict?

It was not the punishment that got the addict into treatment. It was the fact that their family is deeply, emotionally meaningful to the addict. Their family goes to the core of the addict's being, to his self-concept. It is the center of the addict's spiritual life. The addict brought the meaning that his family has for him to bear on the meaning that alcohol and drugs have for him. And his family won!

Yes, the addict may love drugs. But he loves his family more.

Chapter Five: A Group of Addicts We Don't Punish

We stated earlier that the news about addiction is good.

When a family faces addiction, there is every reason to hope their loved one can achieve sobriety through treatment and a strong recovery program. Each year we know more about addiction, more people are coming to treatment, and there are now good medications available to help them stay sober.

The news is good.

Yes, there is still a lot of pessimism out there about addiction.

Many people focus on the likelihood of relapse, and make dire pronouncements about an addict's chances of ever getting sober. But we don't feel this pessimism is warranted.

The truth is: people get sober all the time.

And now we're going to talk about a group of addicts that have phenomenal recovery rates from addiction.

The hope is that your family member can be in that group, too.

When we treat addiction as a disease, and when we remove the punishment from our approach to the addict, things get better. In fact, many of the more difficult problems in addiction medicine simply disappear. Addiction, in turns out, can be a surprisingly easy clinical problem to manage.

If we remove the punishment.

How do we know this?

Well, there is a group of addicts out there that we don't punish.

Sometimes they are severely ill alcoholics. Still, if we find out about their addiction, we don't get angry. We don't threaten them. We don't fire them from their jobs or take away their children. We get them the best treatment—non-punitive treatment—money can buy. And then, when they are better, we return them to their jobs and their family. Amazingly enough, just by taking the anger and punishment out of the equation they come to treatment on their own. They don't need to be coerced. They stay in treatment longer. They do better.

Who are these addicts that we don't punish?

Pilots.

The United States Navy has almost forty years of experience treating alcoholism in their pilots.

They recognized that they had a problem with alcohol abuse in their squadrons. But they noticed that if they took a punitive, zero-tolerance approach, their aviation mishap rate got worse. The alcohol pilot hid himself and the Navy only found out about it when there was an accident.

But the Navy reasoned that if they treated addiction in the pilot not as a moral problem but as a safety problem, if they took the punishment out and allowed pilots to come forward, get treated and return to flying, their mishap rate went down. So the Navy adopted this program in the 1960s, and since then they haven't had a single alcohol-related mishap. Over ninety-percent of the pilots treated for alcoholism return to flying status.

Over ninety percent!

That's the kind of success rate we see if we take out the punishment.

Pilots, you see, have something that is deeply, emotionally meaningful to them: flying. More than any other occupational group, pilots love what they do. Being a pilot goes to the core of their being. Their connection to flying is, well, *spiritual*. Far from stripping of that spiritual meaning, the Navy uses it against the meaning of alcohol.

And flying wins.

Please note: it's not the reward of flying that gets them sober. Nor is it the threat of never flying again that brings them to treatment. It's the fact that their occupational role—being a pilot—is more meaningful to them then alcohol.

Much the way your family is now facing a problem with addiction, the Navy was faced with alcoholism in their pilots. Yes, perhaps the Navy adopted its impaired pilot program because it simply wanted fewer mishaps. But the Navy also values its pilots. In so many ways the Navy tells its pilots that they matter, that their skills are valuable, that it wants to do everything it can to keep them flying. If the pilot develops a problem with alcoholism, well, the Navy insists that he get treatment and get sober. But the Navy will help them, and then get them back to work.

The Navy could not bring itself to punish its pilots because the Navy, not to put it too melodramatically, loves its pilots.

Just as your family loves your addict.

You might think that these pilots get sober because they are so much more intelligent, so much more accomplished, so much more mentally healthy than the average person—and perhaps more than your addict. That is not the reason these pilots get sober.

It's not the qualities of the pilot that get them to bring them to treatment. It's the quality of the message: you matter, your skills are valuable, you are a vital part of this organization, we want to keep you with the thing that you love and gives your life meaning. You have to get sober! How can we help? That's what gets them sober.

We think that message would work on your addict, too: You matter. Your skills are valuable. You are a vital part of this family. We want to keep you with us. You have to get sober!

How can we help?

By the way, the Navy's program was so successful that the commercial airlines adopted it, too. They treat their alcoholic pilots and return them to flying. This is why there hasn't been an alcohol-related commercial aviation accident in thirty years. Your stewardess probably won't mention this to you as you board your aircraft. But these non-punitive, medically-based addiction treatment programs work. And they have now been replicated for doctors, nurses, lawyers, dentists, pharmacists...and all these groups have a greater than eighty percent success rate in treatment.

We want that kind of success rate for your family, too.

When we realize that addiction is a disease, and that addicts are patients, and that they respond to caring treatment just as well as other patients do, suddenly addiction is not that hard. Recovery starts to look like a very real possibility. And for the family, there finally is some hope.

Chapter Six: People Get Sober All The Time

So is addiction a disease?

If we follow our definition that disease is a defect that occurs in an organ that leads to symptoms we should be able to fit addiction easily.

The organ in question is the midbrain. The defect is a stress-induced dysregulation of the brain's hedonic system –its ability to properly perceive pleasure. And the symptoms we observe are as follows: (1) Loss of control—the addict tries mightily to corral their drug use, to cut back, to take a break. They fail with each try. (2) Craving—and intense, emotional obsession with the drug that is true suffering but also, and most importantly, involuntary. And (3) Persistent Drug Use Despite Negative Consequences—perhaps the most upsetting symptom of all, especially to those around the addict. The midbrain equates the drug with survival and so, when stressed, it must do everything it can to get the drug, consequences not withstanding.

So we have the organ, we have the defect, and we have symptoms directly traceable to that defect. We have met the burden of proof: addiction fits the Disease Model! This is why we can—with confidence—say that addiction is, in fact, a disease.

To some, calling addiction a disease may appear to undermine our concept of free will. It is true, what we now know about addiction calls into question many of our long-held and cherished beliefs about the nature of human choice. But addiction also tells us much about how choice actually works, and how the brain's capacity to exercise free will can fail while in disease states.

Addiction is a disorder of volition. Choice, it turns out, is not an all-or-nothing capacity. It varies. Our task is to discover the conditions under which it best operates—when it's strong, and when it flags—and set those conditions to preserve our ability to exercise free will in accordance with our values. We think this new neuroscientific understanding of addiction gives us a deeper understanding of free will. We believe this understanding makes our power of choice an even more precious commodity.

Addiction is a brain disease.

It has some very upsetting symptoms, but they respond quite well to good treatment. Addicts can get sober, and learn how to restore their power of choice. It happens all the time. Above all else, the message of this new research into the disease of addiction is this: there is hope.

Why don't more people know about this research? About the good news concerning addiction? About the pilots and doctors and lawyers who have been getting sober for decades?

We're trying to figure that out ourselves.

That was our point in making this book to get the word out. There really is no reason to be pessimistic about addiction.

People get sober all the time.

Notes

Notes